DESERT
AIR FORCE

DESERT
AIR FORCE

Ian Black

OSPREY
AEROSPACE

Published in 1992 by
Osprey Publishing Limited
59 Grosvenor Street, London W1X 9DA

ISBN 1 85532 192 0

Editor Dennis Baldry
Page design by Paul Kime
Printed in Hong Kong

Front cover Panavia Tornado F.3 interceptor 'Delta Lima' of No 11 Sqn streaks across the Saudi desert. Tornado F.3s were among the first RAF combat aircraft to arrive in the Gulf, forming the air defence element of Operation Granby, the United Kingdom's military response to Iraq's invasion of Kuwait, which was announced on 9 August 1990

Back cover All systems would seem to be go as this Panavia Tornado interdictor of the Royal Saudi Air Force is scrutinized pre-taxi at Dharhan AB. This aircraft is also featured on pages 96–97

Title page Flight Lieutenant Ian Black sweats it out in the front cockpit of a Tornado F.3 during a combat air patrol (CAP) over Saudi Arabia in August 1990

Right Buccaneer break. This ex-Granby S.2B displays the US-developed AVQ-23E Pave Spike laser-designator pod (left inboard station) used to illuminate targets for laser guided bombs (LGBs) dropped from medium level by Tornado GR.1s. The store carried on the right outboard station is an ALQ-101(V)-10 jamming pod. Normally tasked with maritime strike, the Buccaneers of Nos 12 and 208 Sqns and No 237 Operational Conversion Unit are based at RAF Lossiemouth in Scotland. Compared to the roughly equivalent Grumman A-6 Intruder, the Buccaneer suffers from ancient avionics, but is much faster (even with one engine shut down the S.2 can maintain 400 knots) and more manoeuvrable

For a catalogue of all books published by Osprey Aerospace
please write to:

**The Marketing Department, Octopus Illustrated Books,
1st Floor, Michelin House, 81 Fulham Road, London SW3 6RB**

About the author

Flight Lieutenant Ian Black joined the Royal Air Force in October 1979, and between February 1981 and February 1984 he served as a navigator on the Phantom FGR.2 with No 19 Sqn (since disbanded) at RAF Wildenrath in Germany. By the end of his tour with No 19 Sqn he was determined to become a pilot.

After instruction at the Flying Selection Squadron at Swinderby (Chipmunk), No 7 Flying Training School at Church Fenton (Jet Provost), he was awarded his wings in February 1986. This period of training was interrupted by a short tour on Chipmunks with No 6 Air Experience Flight at Abingdon in 1984.

Following the successful completion of his course at No 1 Tactical Weapons Unit at Brawdy between March-August 1986, he was posted to the Lightning Training Flight at Binbrook in September 1986, where he had the distinction of being the last pilot to qualify on Britain's unique supersonic single-seat fighter.

After the Lightning was phased out of RAF service in June 1988, Ian Black began his association with the Panavia Tornado ADV at No 229 OCU, subsequently transferring from Coningsby to the Tornado Fighter Wing at Leeming in North Yorkshire. By the beginning of 1992, Ian Black had accumulated 850 hours on the Tornado F.3 during the course of his service with Nos 11, 23 and 25 Sqns.

Most of the pictures in DESERT AIR FORCE were taken between 31 August and 1 December 1990 while the author was based at Dharhan AB in Saudi Arabia. A completely self-taught photographer, Ian Black's first book, JET COMBAT: HOT AND HIGH – FAST AND LOW, was published by Osprey in 1988. The critically-acclaimed large-format COMBAT EDGE followed in May 1991. Fittingly, he was awarded first prize in the air-to-air category of the annual RAF photographic competition in December 1991.

The photographs in DESERT AIR FORCE were shot using Nikon cameras and lenses, loaded with Fujichrome and Kodak colour-negative film. The views expressed in this book are the author's and do not necessarily reflect those of the UK Ministry of Defence or of the Royal Air Force.

A night training mission beckons as this Bahrain-based Tornado GR.1 awaits its crew. Three squadrons, each with 15 GR.1s, operated from Gulf bases during Desert Storm

Contents

Desert Eagles

Above On 8 August 1990, only six days after the Iraqi invasion of Kuwait, US Air Force F-15C/Ds of the 1st Tactical Fighter Wing arrived at Dhahran Air Base in Saudi Arabia, from where they operated combat air patrols (CAPs) to deter further Iraqi aggression and protect the subsequent build-up of Coalition forces as part of Operation Desert Shield

Left A bandit's eye view of a McDonnell Douglas F-15C Eagle air superiority fighter: the nose radome houses a Hughes APG-70 pulse-Doppler fire control radar, which enabled the aircraft to out-range any adversary in the Iraqi inventory – including the much-vaunted Mikoyan MiG-29 *Fulcrum*

Above Displaying the yellow fin stripe of the 27th Tactical Fighter Squadron, the badge of Tactical Air Command, and 'FF' tailcode of Langley AFB, Virginia this F-15D air superiority fighter trainer of the 1st TFW awaits take-off clearance as a further pair of two-seat Eagles standby in the background. First flown on 19 June 1979, the F-15D retains the full operational capability of the single-seat F-15C. The 600 US gal combat-rated fuel tank under the belly of the aircraft is standard fit, but a further 1500 US gal can be carried in conformal fuel tanks (CFTs) fitted to the sides of the jet intake trunks

Right Engines running, this pair of F-15Cs will start to taxi away from their sunken revetment just as soon as the Eagle pilot in the background has completed his 'full and free movement' control checks and given the OK to pull the wheel chocks. The trusty M61A1 six-barrel 20 mm cannon with up to 940 rounds is carried in the starboard wing root, under which the badge of the 1st TFW is clearly visible on the nearest aircraft

These pages The heat is on as a pilot from the 1st TFW settles into the Eagle's capacious cockpit, donning his HGU-55/P lightweight helmet and oxygen mask prior to energizing the jet. The USAF planned to have the much more 'user friendly' Combat Edge anti-G system issued to F-15 and F-16 units during 1990, but the programme was postponed because of the urgency involved in deploying aircraft to the Gulf. Developed by Boeing Defense & Space Group, the Combat Edge system includes an inflatable Nomex vest worn over standard flight gear and a new low-profile oxygen mask with a tensioning system which is only activated at high-G, so the pilot does not have to endure the mask being uncomfortably tight all the time

Optimized for combat at high-subsonic speeds, the low aspect ratio wing of the F-15 is of deceptively simple form, the moveable surfaces comprising plain flaps and ailerons. Also apparent as this F-15C proceeds purposefully to the runway are the twin vertical tail surfaces (with the red fin stripe of the 71st TFS), the all-moving tailplanes with saw-toothed extended leading-edges and the convergent/divergent nozzles for the Pratt & Whitney F100-PW-220 turbofans, each of which is rated at 23,450 lb of thrust at sea level. To the immense disappointment of more than a few RAF pilots, reports that the service was planning to lease a squadron of F-15s (apparently refurbished A/B models released by the 36th TFW at Bitburg AB in Germany), pending the arrival of the Tornado ADV (Air Defence Variant) came to nothing

Above A revealing close-up of the F-15C assigned to Capt Steve Tate, the pilot who scored the first kill of Desert Storm by fireballing an Iraqi Mirage F.1EQ with a AIM-7M Sparrow AAM in the early hours of 17 January 1990. The bandit was positively identified as hostile by a patrolling Boeing E-3 Sentry AWACS. Had the combat taken place in daylight, Tate could have used the Eagle Eye 'sniperscope' visible to the right of the head-up display in the cockpit. Eagle Eye enables pilots to visually identify targets at ranges in excess of 20 nautical miles, thereby preserving beyond visual range (BVR) kill capability in situations where the rules of engagement demand a 'vis-ident' before firing and your friendly Airborne Warning And Control System is not available. Significantly, almost all of the 30 confirmed kills scored by Eagles against the Iraqi Air Force were achieved with the radar-guided Raytheon AIM-7M Sparrow in BVR engagements

Right Bitter experience in the skies of Southeast Asia re-affirmed that the dogfight was still a significant factor in air combat. Maxims such as 'he who sees his opponent first usually wins', and 'lose sight, lose the fight' must have seemed rather academic to pilots stuck in the cockpits of F-105 Thunderchiefs or F-4 Phantoms, who had about as much all-round view as the driver of a '69 Ford Mustang. In complete contrast the huge blown canopy of the F-15 gives the pilot the best possible chance of acquiring and maintaining a visual track on his quarry. The ACES II zero-zero ejector seat is built by McDonnell Douglas at their Long Beach plant

These pages Gulping Gatoraid was one American answer to the fluid loss caused by the searing desert heat. Allegedly some kind of lime soda, this curious elixir seemed to be the favourite tipple of many F-15 pilots. After tasting the stuff, RAF Tornado crews were distinctly unimpressed and preferred to drink water instead. Carrying half a litre of water out to the aircraft was one of many novelties experienced at Dhahran, but all the bottles would be empty at the end of a four-hour mission

Above A piece to camera (out of shot) for Saudi TV. The Saudis are understandably very proud of their F-15s, being one of only three other operators (with Japan and Israel) of the aircraft apart from the USA. The strip under the ROYAL SAUDI AIR FORCE titling is a low- intensity formation-keeping light. Illuminated at night, these give an immediate indication of the distance, attitude and position of the aircraft to other pilots. Other strips are located on the wingtips and rear fuselage. The RSAF began to take delivery of its Eagles in January 1981, the authorized total of 60 aircraft being handed over by the summer of 1983. During the course of September 1990 a further twelve Eagles were transferred to the RSAF from the USAF's 32nd TFS at Soesterberg AB in the Netherlands, and an equal number from the 36th TFW at Bitburg

Right Aware of rising manpower costs, the USAF stressed the importance of maintainablity in the original specification for the F-15. By the standards of the early seventies, the number of access panels and electronic line-replaceable units (LRUs) was very impressive. After consulting the relevant technical manual, the crew chief sat under the 'beak' of this Eagle will help the rest of the groundcrew to make the aircraft combat ready

Above A former operator of the Lightning F.53, No 13 Sqn now shares Dhahran AB with No 42 Sqn, the RSAF's newest F-15 unit. The other two RSAF Eagle squadrons, Nos 5 and 6, are based at Taif and Khamis Mushayt

Right Inside a hangar purpose-built for the F-15, an F100 turbofan is 'pulled' for overhaul. Developed specifically for the F-15, but subsequently adopted by the F-16, the F100 has a three-stage fan and a 10-stage compressor, with a bypass ratio of 0.7:1. The control levers and rods which adjust the nozzle aperture were originally covered by plates known as 'turkey feathers', these being deleted from the F-15A after aerodynamic and maintenance problems revealed that they were more trouble than they were worth

With plenty of concrete to play with, this Saudi pilot chooses to land his F-15C without using the massive ventral airbrake, although the nose is still held high so as to maximize aerodynamic braking. Configured for a combat air patrol mission, the aircraft is carrying three 600 US gal external tanks, four radar-guided AIM-7M Sparrow AAMs and four infrared-guided AIM-9L Sidewinder AAMs. A RSAF F-15C piloted by Capt Ayedh Salam-Al-Shamrani scored the first double-kill of Desert Storm, when on 24 January 1991 two Iraqi Mirage F.1EQs were splashed by Sidewinders as they attempted to make an Exocet attack against Coalition shipping

Devoid of external stores, a Saudi F-15C watches the dawn rise at Dhahran as other Eagles and RAF Tornado F.3s shelter in the background. RSAF Eagles had seen combat before Desert Storm, having despatched two Iranian F-4E Phantoms which unwisely penetrated Saudi airspace during the course of operations against Iraq in an earlier and appallingly protracted Gulf conflict

The French Connection: Operation Salamandre

Above Normally part of BA115 at Orange-Caritat, EC 2/5 were deployed to Al Ahsa, near Hofuf, some 70 nm south of Dhahran. Casting the unmistakeable shadow of its delta planform, this Mirage 2000C RDI is being refuelled during the turn-around for its next foray along the Saudi/Iraq border

Right Using *postcombustion*, a Dassault-Breguet Mirage 2000C RDI (*Radar Doppler á Impulsion*) interceptor of *Escadron de Chasse* 2/5 'Ile de France' rotates as it begins a practice CAP mission

Above In common with their RAF counterparts, the French
Air Force Mirage 2000 pilots were to be denied the opportunity to meet the
Iraqis in the blue arena. After comprehensive attacks against its air defence
environment and airfields, much of what remained of Saddam Hussein's air
power (about 145 aircraft), ran away to Iran. The French do not design ejection
seats, so the pilot is sitting on a British Martin-Baker F10Q

Right This EC 2/5 *pilote* makes himself as comfortable as possible in the few
minutes remaining before he energizes the Mirage's SNECMA M53P-2
turbofan, which is rated at 21,385 lb of thrust in afterburner at sea level. This
wide-angle view tends to exaggerate the size of the radar radome and the bolt-
on refuelling probe positioned in front of the windscreen. Aircraft recognition
experts will have spotted the row of Jaguar As in the background

Above Although designed to incorporate the latest digital computers and head-up/head-down displays, the cockpit of the 2000 would not seem inordinately strange to pilots of the preceding Mirage III/5/F.1 series. Apart from the one-piece windscreen, the design of the canopy is virtually unchanged. The pilot is wearing his newly- issued desert-camouflaged flying overalls. Sand-coloured helmets were also issued

Right A formidable fighter, the Mirage 2000C RDI is typically armed with two Matra Super 530 D (Doppler) AAMs for long-range attacks, and two Matra R 550 *Magic II* dogfight missiles; the fixed armament is two 30 mm DEFA 554 cannons with 125 rounds each (the muzzle of the starboard cannon is visible under the intake trunk). The 2000C RDI is significantly faster than the F-16 and F/A-18 Hornet, being capable of Mach 2.2 at altitude

The force mix of Operation Salamandre included six Dassault-Breguet Mirage F.1CR reconnaissance aircraft drawn from ER 33e of BA124 at Strasbourg-Entzheim. Housed in a bay behind the black radome for the *Cyrano IVMR* mapping radar (useful for updating the inertial navigation system as required), is a 150 mm Omera 33 vertical camera and a 75 mm Omera 40 camera for panoramic coverage. *Super Cyclope* infrared linescan replaces the starboard DEFA cannon. Outboard of the big 1700-litre external fuel tanks is (left of picture) a *Phimat* chaff dispenser, balanced by a *Barax* ECM pod on the opposite pylon. The first production Mirage F.1CR made its maiden flight on 10 November 1982, and 68 aircraft were subsequently delivered to the *Armée de l'Air Francaise*

Above *Entente cordiale* at Al Ahsa: French Mirage pilots enjoy the company of Isobel Elsen, a photographer from the British daily newspaper, *The Independent*

Left A member of the groundcrew clambers up the ladder to attach 'sized to fit' pieces of silver foil inside the canopy, thereby preventing heat damage to the cockpit. This Mirage F.1CR is fitted with a *Raphael* SLAR (Sideways Looking Airborne Radar) pod on the centreline. The reconnaissance missions mounted by the F.1CRs of ER 33e were supported by imagery from the SPOT satellite and electronic intelligence from a C.160NG *Gabriel* aircraft. In *Tempête du Désert*, F.1CRs utilized their secondary ground attack capability with four 250 kg bombs or two AS 30 Laser missiles

Above Al Ahsa was also home to the Jaguar As of *Escadrille de Chasse* 11, whose 27 aircraft flew 1088 hours in 615 combat sorties during Desert Storm. Most of the wing's Jaguars travelled to Saudi from their base at Toul-Rosières, but some were redeployed from Chad in North Africa, where they had been operating in support of French ground forces to defend the north of the country against pro-Libyan insurgents

Left Evolved from the Breguet Br 121 project, the Jaguar was produced collaboratively by SEPECAT (a company formed by Dassault-Breguet and the British Aircraft Corporation) to fulfil a common *Armée de l'Air Francaise* and Royal Air Force requirement for an advanced trainer and ground attack aircraft. In the event, the type became too expensive to operate in the training role (which led to the development of the Alpha Jet and Hawk), and the two-seat Jaguar E (RAF designation T.2) was given operational capability. The first Jaguar to fly was the advanced trainer prototype E-01, which left the ground on 8 September 1968; the first Jaguar A flew on 23 March 1969. This line-up of suitably protected Jaguar As display their very effective desert camouflage

Above Jaguar groundcrews huddle together so as to confirm the order in which each aircraft is scheduled to start engines and taxi out for the next mission. Behind the glazed panel under the nose of the aircraft is a laser ranger, a device which enables the pilot to drop his bombs with exceptional precision if the target is illuminated by a laser designator

Left In Desert Storm the Jaguar As were armed with four 250 kg bombs (high-explosive or the *Beluga* cluster variety), or two 100 mm rocket pods on the inboard pylons; a *Barax* ECM pod was carried on the port outboard pylon, and a *Magic II* dogfight missile for self-defence on the opposite outboard pylon. A 1200-litre ventral fuel tank was invariably carried unless the mission involved the AS 30 Laser, in which case the external tank was slung under the starboard inboard pylon to balance the missile and the centreline station used by the ATLIS (Automatic Tracking Laser Illumination System) pod. AS 30 Laser attacks were made on 18 January 1990 against the Ras Al Qlhaya ammunition dump 30 km south of Kuwait City, and on 10 February 1990 when the Jaguars cut one of the bridges across the Euphrates. The pilots were issued with hand-held satellite navigation systems which were attached inside the cockpit using strips of velcro

Tornado Air Defence

A self-portrait of the author at work in the front cockpit of a Panavia Tornado F.3 interceptor; both aircraft are breaking out of close formation during a training mission near the Saudi/Iraq border in September 1990. The first twelve Tornado F.3s arrived at Dhahran on 11 August 1990, six aircraft each being provided by Nos 5 and 29(F) Sqns from RAF Akrotiri in Cyprus, where they had been sent for Armament Practice Camp (APC). No 29(F) Sqn had already completed its APC when Iraq invaded Kuwait on 2 August 1990, but No 5 Sqn were only at Akrotiri for a few days before they flew to Saudi Arabia. Known informally as the Coningsby detachment (the Lincolnshire base being the home of both squadrons), the F.3s launched their first CAP from Dhahran on 12 August 1990. In the face of Iraqi belligerence near the Kuwait/Saudi border, the Tornados were a welcome addition to the air defence assets of the Saudis

Right When it became clear that Saddam Hussein had, as General H Norman Schwarzkopf put it, 'missed the bus' and failed to move against Saudi Arabia before the bulk of the Coalition forces were in theatre, the UK MoD took the opportunity to replace the Coningsby aircraft, aircrew and groundcrew with those from RAF Leeming in North Yorkshire, where the author was serving with No 25 Sqn. This Tornado F.3 (ZE968/DJ) is one of the Block 13 aircraft upgraded to Stage 1 Plus standard for Operation Granby (Britain's codename for the Gulf deployment). The modifications included GEC-Marconi Foxhunter radars to Type AA standard, HOTAS (Hands On Throttle And Stick) short-range combat controls and GEC-Marconi Hermes radar homing and warning receivers. Interestingly, a switch located by the throttles enabled the pilot to override the RB.199 Mk 104 turbofans' top-temperature limiters and obtain an extra five per cent combat boost

Below The Granby F.3s were also fitted with two Tracor ALE-40(V) flare dispensers on the engine access panels

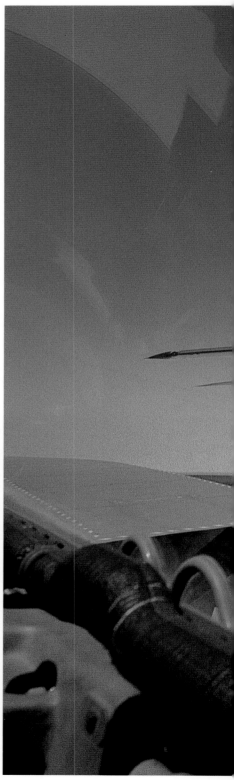

With any luck the seeker of an incoming infrared missile would be decoyed by the juicy target presented by a well-timed flare. However, the best form of defence is attack: Granby F.3s were armed with the latest Sky Flash 90 radar-homing missiles which can be fired at longer ranges than the standard item, and AIM-9M Sidewinder infrared-guided missiles. The four Sky Flash are carried semi-recessed under the fuselage in order to minimize drag

The crew of 'Delta Juliet' look down on Dhahran AB from an altitude of 3000 ft as they prepare for landing. This aircraft is carrying a pair of 1500-litre external tanks, which were only used for training missions. CAPs required the considerable extra range conferred by the 2250-litre 'Hindenbergers'. The DESERT EAGLES – ROYAL AIR FORCE badge on the fin was not generally applied to the Granby F.3s

These pages On 15 September 1990, the OC No 5 Sqn and two crews from No 25 Sqn flew a vic of Tornado F.3s over Dhahran to coincide with the 50th anniversary Battle of Britain flypast by 166 RAF aircraft over London. Although the RAF has been involved in many conflicts since the end of World War 2, the last time an RAF fighter actually shot down an enemy aircraft was in May 1948, when Spitfire Mk 18s of No 208 Sqn despatched five Egyptian Spitfire Mk 9s amid the confusion of the British withdrawal from Palestine. No Tornado F.3 crew doubted that if war came they were bound to engage some of the 700 combat aircraft operated by the Iraqi Air Force, most notably the MiG-29 *Fulcrum*, Su-24 *Fencer* and Mirage F.1EQ. However, despite flying over 360 missions in Desert Storm, the F.3s never managed to get a shot off; nearly half of Iraq's combat aircraft had been either destroyed on the ground or had taken refuge in Iran. The most serious threat proved to be the 23 mm and 57 mm anti-aircraft artillery (AAA) directed at the F.3s when they were at low-level in the CAP operating areas

These pages The almost surreal appearance of the Saudi coastline was a revelation for aircrews accustomed to flying over the often stark, slate grey waters of the North Sea. The sand-coloured 1500-litre plastic tanks fitted to the aircraft pictured at bottom right came off a Tornado GR.1. Developed from the Panavia Tornado IDS (interdictor/strike) version by BAe at Warton in Lancashire, the Tornado interceptor was optimized to counter the threat posed by Soviet long-range strike aircraft like the Sukhoi Su-24 *Fencer* and Tupolev Tu-22M *Backfire*. The F.3 has the endurance, radar, armament, speed (over Mach 2) and manoeuvrability needed to knock down incoming hostile aircraft far away from their targets on the UK mainland (and maritime targets in the North Atlantic and Western Approaches)

Above By the end of August 1990, the artistic talent at Akrotiri had already recorded the involvement of Nos 5 and 29(F) Sqns in Desert Shield. In company with No 43(F) Sqn, No 29(F) Sqn's tour of duty in the subsequent Desert Storm ended when the F.3 detachment ceased flying operations on 8 March 1991

Left The Tornado is the only operational European combat aircraft with a variable geometry wing. Once airborne, the wings are swept back to the 45-degree position seen here, this setting being ideal for most phases of the mission, including visual air combat and flight refuelling. As it generates the most lift, the fully-forward 25-degree setting is always used for take-off/landing and to extend loiter time on CAP if required. The slats and flaps only deploy if the wings are set at 25 or 45-degrees. A supersonic dash requires 67-degrees of sweep, this configuration minimising wave drag/maximising acceleration

Above The business end of one of the many AIM-9M Sidewinder infrared-guided missiles which were rapidly supplied from US Navy stocks for use by the Granby F.3s. Compared to the AIM-9L version built by Bodenseewerk for the RAF and other NATO air forces, the 'Mike' has a cleaner-burning rocket motor and an improved seeker head

Left The F.3's long-range punch is provided by the BAe Sky Flash semi-active radar-homing missile, the rounds being uploaded in tandem pairs under the fuselage. When fired, the missiles are pushed clear of the aircraft by Frazer Nash ejector release units. Developed from the AIM-7E Sparrow, Sky Flash is fitted with an advanced Marconi-designed guidance system which enables it to destroy the most demanding of targets, such as a low-flying aircraft in a heavy ECM environment. Downstream of the missile is a fully-loaded Tracor ALE-40(V) flare dispenser

Above An F.3 confirms that its flight refuelling probe is still serviceable as it taxies in post-mission. CAPs were flown 24-hours a day, the Granby F.3s alternating with RSAF F-15s/F.3s and USAF F-15s

Right Mask unfastened, the pilot heads his F.3 back to its 'sun shelter' after a four-hour CAP mission. The size of the radome for the AI.24 Foxhunter radar is readily apparent. Foxhunter uses a pulse-Doppler technique known as frequency-modulated interrupted continuous wave, its principal benefit being the ability to pick out low-level targets against ground clutter. GEC-Marconi claims that Foxhunter gives the F.3 the longest target acquistion range of any land-based interceptor. Behind the radome in the starboard lower fuselage is the 27 mm Mauser cannon. The space utilized by the second cannon on the Tornado IDS is used to house the avionics displaced by the built-in flight refuelling probe

These and preceding pages At maximum take-off weight (over 61,000 lb) with 'Hindenbergers' and full armament, ZE907 'Delta Kilo' and ZE165 'Delta Uniform' get the benefit of full combat power (approximately 39,000 lb of thrust) from their Turbo-Union RB.199 turbofans. In common with the Tornado GR.1s, the F.3s were given coatings of radar-absorbent material (RAM) on the leading edges of the wing, intake ducts and vertical tail, the stealthy nature of the latter surface being especially clear in the shot on the preceding page

These pages A Granby F.3 leads a echelon starboard formation (above) and brings up the rear of a box formation comprising the RAF's three other fast-jet Gulf players, namely the Buccaneer, Tornado GR.1 and Jaguar. A total of 135 RAF aircraft (including 18 Tornado F.3s, 46 Tornado GR.1/1As, 12 Jaguar GR.1s, and 12 Buccaneer S.2s) flew over 6100 sorties during the course of Desert Storm

RAF Interdictors

One of the estimated 84 Panavia Tornado GR.1/1As interdictor/reconnaissance aircraft to receive the 'Pink Panther' desert camouflage scheme wings its way to the Gulf in September 1990. The first dozen Granby GR.1s left RAF Brüggen on 27 August 1990 and were deployed to Bahrain International Airport (RAF Muharraq until Britain withdrew its forces from east of Suez in the 1960s). Tabuk in far northwestern Saudi Arabia played host to the second Granby GR.1 squadron from 8 October 1990, the aircraft coming from Laarbrüch, but flown by crews from RAF Marham in Norfolk. A third squadron of Brüggen GR.1s arrived at Dhahran on 3 January 1991, followed by a recce element of six GR.1As from Laarbrüch and RAF Honington between 14–16 January. Tabuk later took a further 15 Tornados, seven of which were equipped to carry the ALARM anti-radar missile and tasked with defence suppression. Modifications specific to the Granby GR.1/1As included GPS Navstar receivers and the use of stage 17F single-crystal turbine blades in their RB.199 Mk 103 turbofans, these having initially suffered blade problems due to desert dust forming a glass deposit that clogged the cooling holes

Above 'Pink Panthers' form up for a photo-call during a ferry flight to the Gulf. All of the RAF Tornados selected for Gulf service were equipped with Have Quick 2 secure radios and IFF to Mk 12 Mode 4 cryptographic standard

Right A close-up of GR.1 'Bravo Alpha', one of the Brüggen aircraft deployed to Bahrain. The retractable flight refuelling probe (obligatory for all of the Tornado missions in Desert Storm) is in the extended position next to the canopy. Visible behind the radome is the muzzle of the starboard Mauser 27 mm cannon, under which is the streamlined fairing for the Ferranti LRMTS (Laser Ranger and Marked Target Seeker). Under the belly are two Hunting JP233 airfield attack weapons, each pod containing 30 SG3657 concrete-cratering bomblets and 215 HB876 area-denial mines. A Sidewinder AIM-9 for self-defence is lurking under the stub pylon

Above Night flying was common to interdictor and air defence crews alike, the cloak of darkness being used to great effect until the Iraqi defences were sufficiently weakened. Post-CAP, an F.3 crew from No 25 Sqn look for somewhere to park

Left Dhahran was a Tornado base long before the Granby aircraft arrived in August 1990, interdictor and air defence versions having been supplied to the RSAF by BAe as part of the Al Yamamah programme. Sporting a lightweight Alpha helmet, this Saudi navigator concentrates on his pre-start checks

Tornado GR.1 *Anna Louise* being flown over the Solway Firth on the Scottish borders by a crew from No 31 Sqn at Brüggen in April 1991. The nose art applied by artistically-inclined groundcrew some weeks after the beginning of Desert Storm was subsequently removed when the aircraft returned to the UK

Above The bomb symbols (those with extended noses denoting the use of laser guided bombs) indicate that *Anna Louise* is a veteran of 29 missions in Desert Storm. More tastefully attired than her namesake on the starboard side, this *Anna Louise* is leaning on the access door for the magazine of the port Mauser cannon

Right The Dhahran and Tabuk based Tornados retained the two-letter codes of their donor units, the initials often being used by the servicing crews to assign pet names and add appropriate nose art. Apart from *Anna Louise*, other notable examples were ZD470/DA *Dhahran Annie*, ZD844/DE *Donna Ewin* and ZD851/AJ *Amanda Jane*

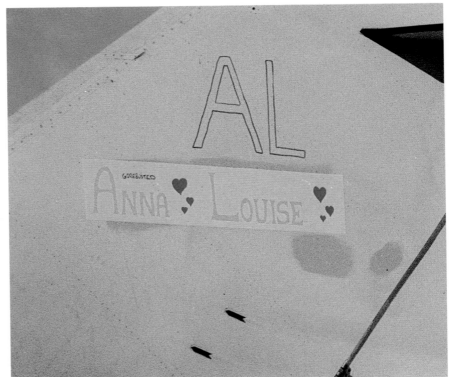

Home from the war, Tornado GR.1 *Anna Louise* roars down the runway in full reheat. Considering the number and complexity of the 1600 sorties flown by the Granby GR.1s in Desert Storm their losses were astonishingly low at just seven aircraft (including one abandoned due to a control restriction shortly after take-off). At 2200 GMT (0100 Local) on 17 January 1990, GR.1s launched the first RAF combat missions of the war. Tallil airfield in southeast Iraq was the target for the JP233s carried by four GR.1s from Dhahran and eight GR.1s from Bahrain. This first wave of the day attacked successfully and returned to their bases without loss, but the second wave from Bahrain ran into trouble when they raided Shaibah, close to the city of Basrah. Flt Lts Adrian 'John' Nicholl and John Peters of No XV Sqn were forced to eject from ZD791 when one of its Sidewinders was detonated by a burst of flak. The pair had to endure considerable mistreatment in captivity

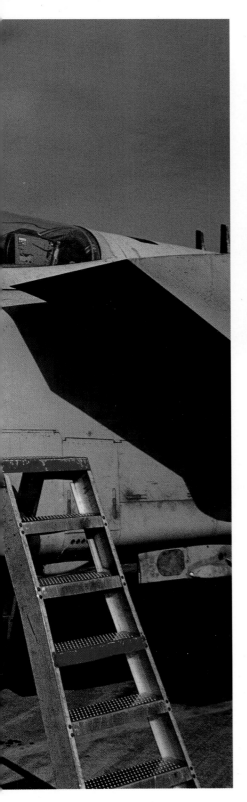

These pages Mission symbols fading and with its 'sharkmouth' no longer visible, Tornado GR.1 ZA466/F of No XV Sqn released its share of the over 800, 1000 lb bombs used by the unit during more than 200 Desert Storm sorties. Before it received desert camouflage, ZA466 bore the MacRobert crest on the nose, No XV Sqn's association with the family dating back to World War 2 when Lady MacRobert donated a Short Stirling bomber (*MacRobert's Reply*) to the RAF after one of her sons was killed on operations. Her two remaining sons also flew with RAF Bomber Command – tragically, they too perished before Germany was defeated. No XV Sqn was disbanded as an operational unit at RAF Laarbrüch in September 1991, part of the planned reduction in the RAF's front-line strength made possible by the collapse of the Warsaw Pact and the warming of relations between the former Soviet Union and the West

One of Tabuk's 'sharkmouthed' GR.1s, *Mig EATER* was credited with destroying a MiG-29 *Fulcrum* (or a Mirage F.1EQ) on the ground in a JP233 attack on 17 January 1991. Two GR.1s which accompanied the initial wave from Tabuk against Al Asad airfield made the first use of ALARMs (Air Launched Anti-Radar Missiles) for defence-suppression. The mission symbols carried by *Mig EATER* give a good indication of the pattern of GR.1 operations against Iraq: JP233 attacks against airfields; lofting ('toss bombing') 1000 lb bombs for defence-suppression and to hit fuel/ammunition dumps, petro-chemical plants, barracks and radar sites; and finally the use of laser-guided bombs to take out hardened aircraft shelters (HASs) and drop bridges

The Tornado GR.1 with the highest number of sorties in Desert Storm was ZA465/FK *FOXY KILLER*, her 44 mission symbols not including five LGB strikes cancelled after take-off due to cloud cover obscuring the target. The aircraft dropped about 100 tons of ordnance over Iraq, comprising four JP233 containers, 158 'dumb' 1000 lb bombs and 35 'smart' 1000 lb laser-guided bombs (actually 1210 lb including the Paveway guidance head and fin). FOXY KILLER is displaying her charms on the pan at RAF Leeming, hence the Tornado F.3 of No 11 Sqn at the end of the line-up

These pages The Tornado GR.1s based at Dhahran had their operational missions marked with palm trees instead of the traditional bomb silhouettes. *Miss Behavin'* leads another GR.1 from No 31 Sqn (repainted in standard camouflage and full squadron markings with its mission markings re-applied) down Leeming's concrete as the pair start their journey back to RAF Brüggen

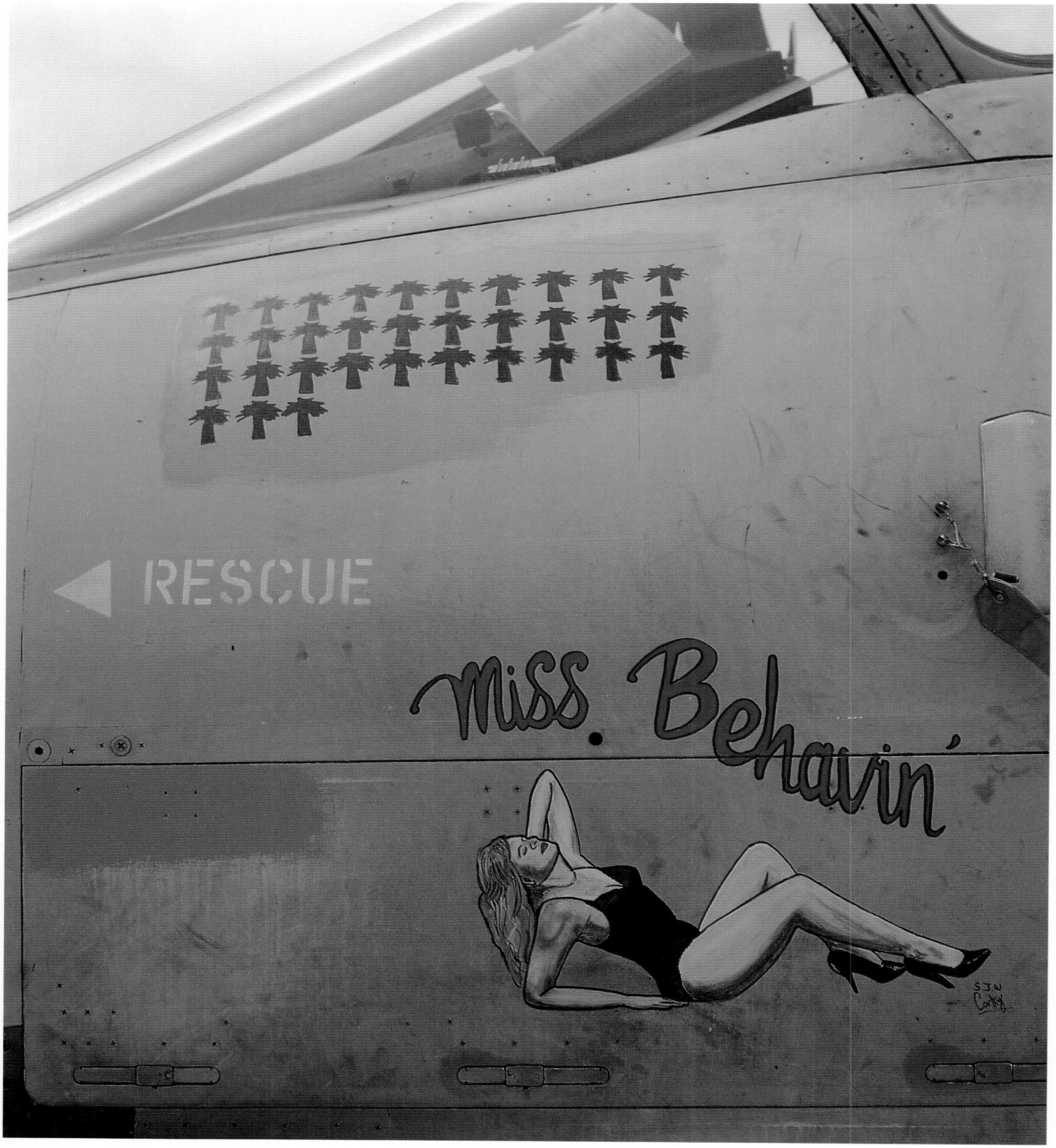
RESCUE
Miss. Behavin'

Above Stormbirds amid the hardened aircraft shelters of the Tornado Fighter Wing at RAF Leeming. A few months before this shot was taken in the spring of 1991, these Tornados had helped to reduce Iraq's HAS population by 64 per cent

Left *Miss Behavin'* was part of the Dhahran Tornado GR.1 detachment which dropped 14 JP233 containers and over a thousand bombs for the loss of a single aircraft. On 23 February 1991, Plt Off Simon Burgess and his navigator, Sqn Ldr Bob Ankerson, were downed by the premature explosion of one their own bombs. The pair ejected successfully and were made PoWs, subsequently being released with the remaining RAF prisoners on 5 March 1991

Above The rear cockpit of the Tornado GR.1 is the heart of the navigation and weapons system. The circular moving map display is flanked by two large multi-function TV tabs (tabulated displays) which can present any alpha-numeric information regarding the aircraft's weapons and systems (eg stores status, fuel remaining and radio frequencies) as required. The joystick visible at the bottom of the instrument panel is part of the attack radar aiming system

Right *Garfield* rides a paper aeroplane, 'flying high' on the forward fuselage of an ex-Dhahran Tornado GR.1 from No 20 Sqn

Above *Miss Behavin'* briefly wore the unique tailcode 'CNN' at Dhahran until the authorities decided that it was inappropriate for an RAF aircraft to advertise Ted Turner's Cable News Network. The store next to the wing tank is a Sky Shadow ECM pod, which always augments the BOZ-107 chaff/flare dispenser carried on the opposite outboard pylon (see page 62)

Right Designed by Blackburn Aircraft in the late fifties as a carrier-borne aircraft optimized for high-speed, low-level nuclear strike, the Buccaneer made its RAF combat debut in Desert Storm. Though they performed superbly, the few Ferranti TIALD (Thermal Imaging and Laser Designation) pods rushed into service for the 'pathfinder' Tornados were inadequate to meet the growing demand for LGB strikes, so on 23 January 1990 RAF Lossiemouth in Scotland was detailed to send six Buccaneer S.2Bs with their Pave Spike laser-designation systems to the Gulf. By 8 February 1990, a full squadron of 12 S.2Bs were in theatre and marking targets for the Tornado detachments at Dhahran and Bahrain. *SEA WITCH/ DEBBIE*, XV863/S took part in six of the 218 Pave Spike sorties in which 169 LGBs were dropped (48 by Buccaneers, these missions being denoted by a red bomb symbol instead of a black one)

Above The Jaguar GR.1A squadron detailed for Operation Granby left their base at RAF Coltishall in Norfolk on 11 August 1990, bound for Thumrait in Oman. This shot of a Jaguar in training fit was taken at Bahrain International Airport, the detachment having moved there in October. In mid-November, the JagDet pilots were rotated with new arrivals from 'Colt', closely followed by the replacement aircraft which would be flown in battle. The most obvious modification to the 'Desert Cats' were the overwing launch rails to carry AIM-9L/M Sidewinders for self-defence, an arrangement which allowed the outer underwing pylons to be occupied by a Westinghouse ALQ(V)-101 radar jamming pod (outer port) and a Phimat chaff dispenser

Left Cat's lair. The 22 JagDet pilots were drawn from Nos 6, 41(F) and 54(F) Sqns at Coltishall and No 226 Operational Conversion Unit at Lossiemouth (the unit and location which received the RAF's first production Jaguar GR.1 in 1973). JagDet pilots flew nearly 922 combat flying hours in 617 sorties during Desert Storm

Above Unlike the Saudi Tornado GR.1 front-seater seen here, the JagDet pilots did not have the benefit of a navigator to help share the high-cockpit workload. Tasked primarily with battlefield air interdiction (BAI), the JagDet usually launched two eight-aircraft attack waves each day, mostly against targets to the south of Kuwait City until the ground war (Desert Sabre) commenced on 22 February, at which point Republican Guard forces to the north occupied most of the 'kill zones'

Top right Its desert camouflage as yet untarnished by wartime operations, a Jaguar GR.1A 'yanks and banks' to reveal the underwing defensive aids mentioned on page 85 and the ALE-40(V) flare scabs fitted under the engines. The spoof canopy created by painting the nosewheel doors black was intended to disguise the true flight path of the aircraft in a dogfight, thereby confusing the enemy pilot. Once in the Gulf, a more convincing effect was produced by silhouetting the canopy exactly

Below right The Jaguar is a handsome aircraft, but its lines inevitably suffer when external stores are added. The distinctive chisel nose with glazed panels houses the Laser Ranger and Marked Target Seeker (LRMTS). Radar warning receivers contained in the long fin-tip fairing provide 360-degree coverage

These pages Two post-Granby views of a No 41(F) Sqn GR.1A safely back on
the pan at RAF Coltishall in the spring of 1991. The nose art applied to XZ364
depicts Iraqi President Saddam Hussein on the receiving end of a British boot.
In the background of the photo on the opposite page is the fin of a non-Granby
Jaguar displaying No 41 Sqn's Cross of Lorraine motif

Above Until Desert Storm, Jaguar pilots only flew above tree-top (some would say hedge-top!) height if they had to refuel or (as here) ferry their aircraft to a distant detachment. The Jaguars were able to operate at medium altitude — beyond the reach of all but the heaviest calibre triple-A — at a very early stage in the campaign due to the masterly suppression of Iraqi air defences by support aircraft such as the EF-111A Raven jamming platform, F-4G Wild Weasel SAM-killer, E-3 Sentry AWACS and the EC-103E ABCCC (Airborne Battlefield Command and Control Centre) operated by the USAF. At the end of the conflict, Iraqi radar emissions had been reduced by 95 per cent

Right XZ106 was one of the JagDet aircraft configured for reconnaissance operations, three such sorties being indicated by SLR camera symbols. Their primary objective was to obtain pre-attack photos of target areas for use by the Reconnaissance Interpretation Centre (RIC). The two Jaguars assigned to this role usually flew as a pair, one aircraft carrying a high-resolution Vinten LOROP (long-range oblique photography) pod, the other an F126 survey camera to compensate for the Vinten unit's narrow field of view and lack of a data matrix

These pages The white-haired pilot flying the pink Spitfire on the nose of Jaguar XX733 could well refer to Sqn Ldr David Bagshaw, a 54-year-old fast jet veteran who logged his 4000th hour on Jaguars on 8 January 1991. Sqn Ldr Bagshaw had five bombing missions to his credit during the initial phase of Desert Storm, as well as a number of solo reconnaissance sorties

Above A post-Granby shot of Jaguar XZ367 'White Rose' being trailed by an F.3 from the Tornado Fighter Wing at RAF Leeming

Right XZ118 displays its contribution to the 750 thousand-pounders, 385 CBU-87 Rockeye IIs, 8 BL755 CBUs (cluster-bomb units), 608 CRV-7 2.75 in rockets and 9600 rounds of 30 mm cannon ammunition expended by the JagDet in Desert Storm. The Sidewinder symbol presumably indicates a missile used against a ground target, as the Iraqi Air Force never came anywhere near the Jaguars

Arabian Attackers

Right Panavia Tornado IDS (interdictor/strike) aircraft were supplied to the Royal Saudi Air Force by British Aerospace under the *Al Yamamah* Phase 1 programme. This immaculate example is displaying its retractable, telescopic flight refuelling probe. As indicated earlier in the text, the FR probe is detachable on the Tornado IDS, but permanent on the ADV

Above Another close-up of the same aircraft, this time revealing its extended airbrakes on the rear fuselage and four of the eight live 1000 lb bombs slung under the belly. Saudi Tornados were not equipped with laser-guided bombs or JP233 airfield attack weapons, which obviously limited their targeting options *vis á vis* the RAF Tornado GR.1s

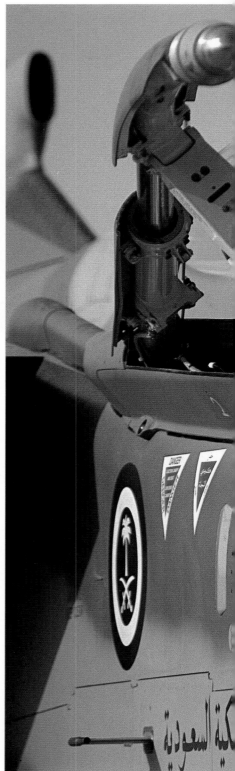

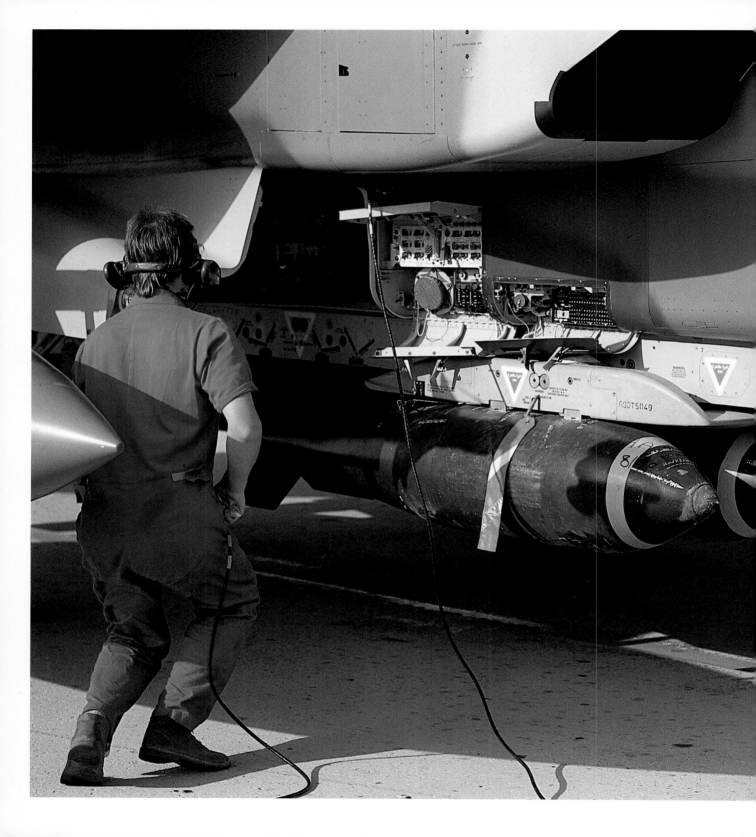

Above Detail of RSAF Tornado IDS number 6602 of No 7 Sqn, based at Dhahran (King Abdul Aziz AB). This squadron was initially formed using Tornados ordered for the RAF, a total of 20 aircraft being diverted from the production line at BAe Warton as required. All Saudi aircrews are trained at the King Fisal Air Academy at Riyadh, which operates Cessna 172s, Pilatus PC-9s, BAe Hawks and BAe Jetstream 31s. Navigators selected for the Tornado IDS receive specific instruction on the J31 using working replicas of the interdictor/strike aircraft's rear cockpit

Left A BAe technician checks the Tornado's CMP (Central Management Panel) for any faults prior to taxi clearance. If all is well, he will remove any remaining safety tags from weapons pylons, etc, before marshalling the aircraft away from the pan. On this practice mission, the Tornado dropped eight 1000 lb retarded bombs (which deploy parachutes after release to slow them down, allowing the aircraft to escape the debris hemisphere of the explosions), in a classic, high-speed/low-level attack

Above The Officer Commanding No 9 Sqn, Kuwait Air Force, pre-flights his McDonnell Douglas A-4KU Skyhawk attack aircraft

Left Some of reportedly 19 A-4KUs which were operating from Dhahran in late-1990. Before the invasion of Kuwait on 2 August 1990, both A-4KU squadrons (Nos 9 and 25) were based at Ahmad al Jabir in the south of the country. After their airfield was bombed the Skyhawks continued combat operations from a stretch of highway, but on 4 August the pilots elected to fly their aircraft to Saudi Arabia in order to prevent them from being captured or destroyed by the advancing Iraqis

Left Strapped into his Escapac 1C-3 rocket ejection seat, a *Free Kuwait* pilot waits for the ground power unit to be connected before spooling up the A-4KU's Pratt & Whitney J52-P-408A turbojet. Equivalent to the A-4M Skyhawk II produced for the US Marine Corps, the A-4KU incorporates an angle-rate bombing system (ARBS), head-up display, enlarged canopy, cranked flight refuelling probe (starboard side), ram-air turbogenerator and braking parachute. The hump-back spine contains avionics. Kuwait Air Force aircraft were not allowed to carry ordnance until Desert Storm began lest their pilots were unable to resist the desire to strike back at Iraq. The soot produced by firing number 802's 20 mm Mk 12 cannon (protruding from the wing root) is evidence of strafing attacks against Iraqi invasion forces

Below Three A-4KUs prepare to hurtle down Dhahran's main runway one after the other, forming-up with their already airborne leader as a four-ship formation

Above Produced by a design team led by the great Ed Heinemann as a carrier-borne attack bomber for the US Navy, the Skyhawk first flew in prototype form on 22 June 1954. The last production Skyhawk (number 2960) was delivered to the Fleet on 27 February 1979. For a bomber the Skyhawk was incredibly compact and much faster than many contemporary fighters (on 14 October 1955 the A4D-1 set a world speed record for a 500 km closed course of 695.163 mph). The long-travel nosewheel landing gear, variable-incidence tailplane and automatic wing slats of this taxiing A-4KU are testimony to the demands imposed by carrier operations

Right The wing's the thing in aircraft design. The Skyhawk's 'cropped' delta planform combined strength with an exceptionally low thickness/chord ratio as well as eliminating the need for wing folding – a great weight saver. As the wing was so thin, the main landing gears had to be accommodated in streamlined fairings. Other excrescences under the wing of this A-4KU are the inboard and outboard pylons, the hardpoints being stressed to 2250 and 1000 lbs respectively

Above Some of the 30 BAe Hawk Mk 65s combat-capable advanced trainers delivered to the RSAF were assigned to the close support role, but it remains unclear whether the aircraft took any active part in Desert Storm. This Hawk is armed with the standard 30 mm Aden cannon pod under the fuselage

Left Skyhawk and Tornado, ground-pounder greeting air-defender as the aircraft recover to Dhahran (bottom left of picture). The Kuwait Air Force received a total of thirty single-seat A-4KUs and six two-seat TA-4KU trainers under a US $250 million fixed-price contract (including spares, support equipment and training) signed on 7 November 1974. In contrast, the cost of 40 F-18C/D Hornets required by the KAF amounted to US $1.9 billion when the contract was signed in August 1988. The first KAF Hornet was delivered in December 1991

Transports and Tankers

The Lockheed C-5 Galaxy heavy logistics transport is the pride of USAF Military Airlift Command (MAC), its global deployment capability having been proven in Vietnam, the Middle East and transatlantic reinforcement exercises on behalf of NATO. First flown on 30 June 1968, the C-5 remained the world's largest military aircraft until the appearance of the Soviet Antonov An-124 *Condor* in December 1982. MAC currently operates around 120 Galaxies, the 50 C-5Bs ordered in 1982 having the extended-life wing and uprated TF30-GE-1C turbofans retrospectively fitted to the remaining C-5As

Above The gargantuan Galaxy is loaded through an upward-hingeing nose and drop-down rear fuselage ramp. By the beginning of Desert Storm, C-5s had transported about 250,000 US tons of cargo to the Gulf

Right Although the C-5 invariably utilizes miles of concrete to take-off and land, its 28-wheel landing gear was designed to permit operations from semi-prepared runways close to the combat zone. Politically, the most valuable missions flown by the C-5 in Desert Storm was the emergency deployment of US Army Patriot missile systems to defend Israel against Iraqi Scud attacks

Above The Lockheed C-141B StarLifter partnered the C-5A/B Galaxy during the massive airlift between the United States and the Gulf. This StarLifter from the 438th Military Airlift Wing at McGuire AFB, New Jersey was one of 265 C-141Bs that took part in Desert Shield/Desert Storm

Left Resplendent in classic MAC markings, a C-141B from the 60th Military Airlift Wing at Travis AFB, California cools out with its groundcrew during a brief pause in airlift operations. The flight deck quarterlights and roof-mounted escape hatch have been opened to help ventilate the aircraft. The all-important flight refuelling receptacle (necessary to maximize payload/range performance) is housed in the fairing aft of the cockpit above the fuselage pressure shell. FR capability was added during the StarLifter conversion programme, which involved stretching most of the original fleet of 285 C-141As delivered between 1965–68 to increase cargo capability by 35 per cent

MAC assets were supplanted by commercial transports during Desert Shield, the first major test of America's Civil Reserve Air Fleet (CRAF) programme. Aircraft such as this McDonnell Douglas DC-8–63CF of Kalitta moved 60–65 per cent of the passengers and 20–25 per cent of the cargo in the US airlift prior to Desert Storm

A USAF veteran, this Boeing C-135B VIP transport serves with the 89th Military Special Missions Wing at Andrews AFB, Maryland – home of the Presidential Flight, callsign 'Air Force One'. One of 30 C-135Bs delivered to the Military Air Transport Service (forerunner of Military Airlift Command) between January and August 1962, the aircraft was configured to Special Air Mission (SAM) requirements in 1968

Above The Lockheed TriStar is by far the largest aircraft ever operated by the RAF. Officially formed at Brize Norton in Oxfordshire on 15 August 1983, No 216 Sqn currently operates a fleet of eight TriStar 500s: four KC.1 tanker/strategic transports, two K.1 dedicated tankers (all ex-British Airways) and two C.2 passenger transports (ex-Pan Am). Under the vigilant gaze his wingman, a Tornado F.3 tops up from a TriStar KC.1 over Egypt en route for Dhahran AB

Right Going home. After taking this study of TriStar ZD952 (ex-G-BFCE), the author boarded the aircraft for the six-hour, 3120-mile non-stop flight from King Khaled International Airport, Riyadh to RAF Brize Norton

Overleaf Mixed formations are all in a day's work for tanker crews, but at present the TriStar is limited by not having the three-point refuelling configuration of the VC10 K.2/3 and Victor K.2. Plans to fit refuelling pods to the wings were complicated by the TriStar 500s active ('fly-by-wire') ailerons, which would have had to be divided as part of the work to attach the pod mounting pylons

Initially there was some concern that the TriStar's low centre engine efflux position (as compared to the equivalent KC-10 Extender, next page) would prove unacceptable for centreline refuelling, but formation flight trials evidently dispelled the doubters. Two hose drum units (HDUs) are incorporated for redundancy, as over-enthusiastic receivers can damage drogues with probes. The TriStar has a total refuelling capacity of 313,300 lb carried in seven fuel tanks in the fore and aft baggage compartments. During the four weeks of the air war one of the TriStar K.1s dispensed 1,325,465 lb of fuel. UK taxpayers will be relieved to know that all the fuel consumed by Coalition forces in Desert Storm was given freely by Saudi Arabia or paid for by Japan

Above and right The McDonnell Douglas KC-10 Extender strategic tanker/transport is equipped with a 'fly-by-wire' Advanced Aerial Refuelling Boom (AARB) for USAF operations; but uniquely the KC-10 also has an integral HDU (right of centreline) to refuel probe-equipped aircraft such as the author's Tornado F.3. A total of seven rubberized fuel bladders (capacity 348,973 lb) are carried in the under deck, three fore and four aft of the wings. The main deck cargo hold (cubic capacity 12,000 ft) can swallow up to 30 standard 9 ft × 7 ft 4 in USAF 463L pallets, or 22 larger units. Derived from the DC-10 Series 30 jetliner, the first KC-10 was flown on 12 July 1980. After helping to deploy fighter wings and other Tactical Air Command assets during Desert Shield, the 59 KC-10s conducted frequent resupply missions between the USA and the Gulf as well as providing dedicated tanker support for Air Force and Navy aircraft in Desert Storm

Above The nine VC10K tankers of No 101 Sqn based at RAF Brize Norton gave magnificent service in the Gulf. Until the outbreak of Desert Storm, the VC10Ks were primarily tasked with CAP support for RAF Tornado F.3 (as here) and Saudi Tornado ADV interceptors, but from an early stage in the conflict this role was usually performed by the 'Pink Pig', No 216 Sqn's desert camouflaged TriStar. Operating from King Khalid International Airport at Riyadh, the VC10Ks flew a total of 1350 combat hours in 381 sorties, many of which required the tankers to orbit close to, or inside, Iraqi airspace. Heavily-laden Tornado GR.1 bombers needed two refuellings inbound to the target and one on return; other customers included US Navy F-14 Tomcat fighters and EA-6B Prowler electronic warfare aircraft involved in strike support

Right The flight deck of the VC10 C.1 transport in which the author travelled out to Gulf from RAF Leeming on 30 August 1990. Autopilot engaged, the captain takes his turn to monitor the flight and handle the radio calls, while the co-pilot concentrates on a story in *The Daily Telegraph* headlined, 'King Hussein leads push for West and Iraq to withdraw'. The last of fourteen VC10 C.1s ordered for the RAF was delivered in 1968 to No 10 Sqn at RAF Brize Norton; the aircraft are named individually after holders of the Victoria Cross

Overleaf A VC10K feeding the author's Tornado F.3

Both wing pods are routinely used together, as demonstrated by VC10 K.3 ZA147/F and two Tornado F.3s. The flight engineer on board the tanker is responsible for monitoring the fuel flow, ensuring that centre of gravity limits are not exceeded during the offload of fuel or when receiving it from another tanker. In the pre-contact position the pilot sees red and amber lights on the centreline fairing or wing pods, indicating that fuel is ready but not available. When the red light is switched off by the flight engineer, the receiver has permission to make contact with the drogue. A good contact is registered after the initial 'prod' when the drogue is pushed a short way forward by the probe; fuel is then passed down the hose, signified by the amber light turning to green. When the receiver has the allotted amount of fuel, the flow is stopped and the green light reverts to amber, signalling the receiver to break off from the drogue. Once contact is broken the lights go to red until the contact area is clear